AF228533

INSIDE MLS

NEW YORK
CITY FC

BY ANTHONY K. HEWSON

SportsZone

An Imprint of Abdo Publishing
abdobooks.com

abdobooks.com

Published by Abdo Publishing, a division of ABDO, PO Box 398166, Minneapolis, Minnesota 55439. Copyright © 2022 by Abdo Consulting Group, Inc. International copyrights reserved in all countries. No part of this book may be reproduced in any form without written permission from the publisher. SportsZone™ is a trademark and logo of Abdo Publishing.

Printed in the United States of America, North Mankato, Minnesota
052021
092021

Cover Photo: Robin Alam/Icon Sportswire/AP Images
Interior Photos: Dennis Schneidler/Icon Sportswire/AP Images, 4–5, 9, 10, 13, 25, 28; Rich Graessle/Icon Sportswire/AP Images, 6, 36; Richard Drew/AP Images, 15; Chuck Zoeller/AP Images, 16; Bryan Smith/Zuma Press/Newscom, 21; Frank Franklin II/AP Images, 18–19, 42; Seth Wenig/AP Images, 23; Fred Kfoury III/Icon Sportswire/AP Images, 26; Dorn Byg/Cal Sport Media/AP Images, 30; Joe Petro/Icon Sportswire/AP Images, 32; Peter Morgan/AP Images, 35; Nam Y. Huh/AP Images, 38; Mark Smith/ZUMA Press/Newscom, 41

Editor: Patrick Donnelly
Series Designer: Dan Peluso

Library of Congress Control Number: 2020948185

Publisher's Cataloging-in-Publication Data

Names: Hewson, Anthony K., author.
Title: New York City FC / by Anthony K. Hewson
Description: Minneapolis, Minnesota : Abdo Publishing, 2022 | Series: Inside MLS | Includes online resources and index.
Identifiers: ISBN 9781532194795 (lib. bdg.) | ISBN 9781098214456 (ebook)
Subjects: LCSH: New York City FC (Soccer team)--Juvenile literature. | Soccer teams--Juvenile literature. | Professional sports franchises--Juvenile literature. | Professional sports franchises--Juvenile literature. | Sports Teams--Juvenile literature.
Classification: DDC 796.334--dc23

TABLE OF CONTENTS

CHAPTER 1

NEW YORK
TURNS BLUE

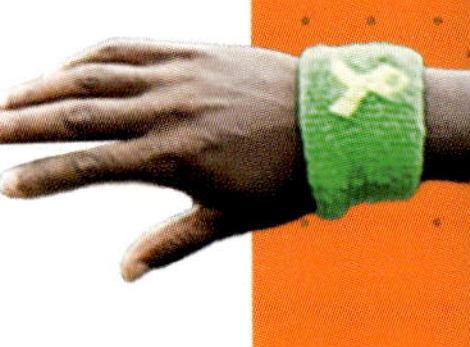

In soccer tradition, a match between two bitter rivals—particularly ones from the same city—is called a derby. Since beginning in 2015, the Hudson River Derby has proven to be one of the most heated rivalries in Major League Soccer (MLS).

New York City Football Club (FC) joined the league in 2015. The team often called NYCFC plays at Yankee Stadium in the Bronx, one of New York City's five boroughs. The New York Red Bulls, meanwhile, had been founded in 1996 and play in Harrison, New Jersey.

On July 3, 2016, a crowd of 33,613 met at Yankee Stadium for the derby's latest installment. Most were dressed in light blue, the color of the home team. A swath of red-clad

NYCFC forward David Villa, right, tries to get past New York Red Bulls defender Chris Duvall.

The addition of Frank Lampard showed that NYCFC was eager to compete immediately.

Red Bulls fans took their seats in the upper deck. The teams had only been rivals for a little more than a season, but their fans already didn't like each other. As kickoff neared, the fans sang and chanted, eager to show the other side who was better. They were playing for the pride of New York City.

BAD BLOOD RISING

Even before the first Hudson River Derby, bad blood existed between the teams' supporters. Many Red Bulls fans believed NYCFC shouldn't even exist. After all, New York City already had a team, and it had been part of MLS from the start. The Red Bulls, originally known as the New York/New Jersey MetroStars, had been playing since 1996, the league's first season.

NYCFC also arrived in MLS with a lot of fanfare. People were curious about this new team, which was owned by the group that owned English powerhouse Manchester City. Few MLS teams could match NYCFC's star power, with world-class players such as David Villa, Frank Lampard, and Andrea Pirlo on the roster. NYCFC was also the first MLS team to play in the city. The Red Bulls had always been based across the river in New Jersey.

All of that interest showed up in the box office. Only two teams in 2015 drew more fans to their home games than NYCFC. Their average crowd of 29,016 was nearly 10,000 more than the Red Bulls managed—though it's worth noting that the Red Bulls played in a much smaller stadium. Still, NYCFC fans enjoyed the opportunity to tweak their more established rivals.

"I think there's a lot of jealousy there that their team, which has been there much longer, wasn't getting that sort of support," explained one member of the Third Rail, NYCFC's main supporters' group.

There was one problem for the new guys. The results on the field skewed steeply to the old guard. In 2015 the Red Bulls won all three meetings with NYCFC, outscoring the expansion team 7–2. The low point for NYCFC came the next year. On May 21, 2016, in the first Hudson River Derby of the season, the Red Bulls came to Yankee Stadium and walloped NYCFC 7–0.

One reporter for the *Guardian* called the home team's performance "a farce. A complete embarrassment." The victory was "embarrassingly easy," said the *New York Times*. But NYCFC captain Villa might have summed it up best: "It was a disaster for us," he said. Thankfully for NYCFC, the next Hudson River Derby was less than two months away.

GAME TIME

This time, meeting just before Independence Day in 2016, NYCFC came out fast. In the eighth minute, Pirlo sent a looping corner kick to the top of the penalty area. At first the ball looked like it was going to no one. Then hotshot rookie Jack Harrison showed up. The English midfielder raced forward to

NYCFC goalkeeper Josh Saunders, *center*, doesn't shy away from contact as he makes a save against the Red Bulls.

Jack Harrison reacts after scoring the first goal of the match.

meet the ball off the bounce. Two defenders thought he was going to slow down and control the ball. Instead Harrison cut toward the goal and blasted a shot with the outside of his right foot, beating Red Bulls goalkeeper Luis Robles on the near post.

"We've been preparing for this game for a long time—it's not just this last week," Harrison said after the match. "We were definitely up for it today."

In the history of the rivalry, NYCFC had led for just 26 minutes. Behind the strong midfield play of Lampard and Pirlo, the team fought to increase that number. As the game went on, though, the Red Bulls began gaining some momentum.

In the 63rd minute, the visitors nearly tied it. Felipe found himself wide open in front of NYCFC's net, yet he still sent his header wide. Three minutes later, NYCFC made them pay.

Harrison, charging up the right sideline, sliced a perfect diagonal pass around two defenders and right to Villa. The Spaniard flicked the ball into the net to double the home team's advantage.

With a 2–0 lead, NYCFC now needed to hold on. The crowd at Yankee Stadium got louder and louder as the clock ticked closer to 90 minutes. A red card was shown to the Red Bulls' Chris Duvall in the 79th minute, building the anticipation further. With a man advantage the rest of the way, NYCFC safely played out the clock as fans sang and chanted.

"For me, three points is three points every game," Villa said, referring to the points his club earned in the standings for the victory. "But for our supporters, this game is a little different, and we're happy for them."

The win sent NYCFC into first place in the Eastern Conference. More importantly, though, the team had notched its first victory in the Hudson River Derby. It was a sign of things to come. NYCFC had come into the league with great expectations, and the 2016 season showed the squad was ready to live up to them, not just against the Red Bulls but against the entire league.

Teammates swarm David Villa (7) after the Spanish striker put NYCFC up 2–0.

BUILDING AN
EMPIRE

Many places claim to be the birthplace of American soccer. But as far as professional soccer goes, few have as strong of an argument as New York. The American Soccer League (ASL) was the country's first major pro soccer league. It was founded at the Astor Hotel in New York City in 1921.

Like a lot of early pro soccer leagues, the ASL didn't last long. The league folded in 1933. But interest in soccer never waned in New York.

NYCFC wasn't the first soccer team to bring major international stars to the Big Apple. The New York Cosmos played their first season in the North American Soccer League (NASL) in 1971. Before MLS, the NASL was the most successful attempt at establishing a major pro soccer league

Pelé and the Cosmos were the face of the NASL in the mid-1970s.

Giorgio Chinaglia led the Cosmos in scoring seven years in a row.

in the United States and Canada. And the Cosmos were the league's most iconic franchise.

The team's owners spent big to lure some of the brightest stars in soccer to New York. Defender Franz Beckenbauer was fresh off winning the World Cup as captain of West Germany. High-scoring Italian striker Giorgio Chinaglia piled up the goals. And the greatest of them all, Brazil's legendary forward Pelé, finished his unparalleled career with the Cosmos.

The Cosmos boasted a collection of stars as famous as just about any in the world—and New Yorkers could watch them in their backyard. The Cosmos drew thousands to their matches at Giants Stadium, with the occasional sellout putting more than 77,000 people in the seats.

The club was the most successful in the NASL, winning five championships. But after Pelé and other stars retired, the Cosmos suffered on and off the field. Financial problems forced the club to fold along with the rest of the NASL after the 1984 season.

THE MLS ERA

With a long history of New Yorkers supporting the game, there was no question the New York area would be part of MLS from

its start in 1996. The team's owners thought about reviving the Cosmos nickname. Instead they decided to name the team the New York/New Jersey MetroStars. Because they would play in New Jersey but also represent New York, both place names were included.

In 2006 the MetroStars were purchased by the Red Bull company and became the New York Red Bulls. It planned to stay in New Jersey and built a new stadium. But as part of the

Over the years, Yankee Stadium hosted many international friendlies, such as this one between Liverpool and Manchester City in 2014.

deal, Red Bull gave up its exclusive rights over the New York metro area. That opened up the city for the establishment of a second MLS team, something the league wanted to happen.

As early as 2007, the league approached some possible owners. It also reached out to the new version of the Cosmos that played in a minor league. But nobody had the interest or the money until 2013.

Meanwhile a group of wealthy investors bought English Premier League club Manchester City in 2008, instantly making that team one of the richest in the world. Four years later, City won its first English league title in 44 years. And in 2013, that ownership group decided to buy into MLS too. They partnered with the New York Yankees baseball team. The team would play games at Yankee Stadium. The new team would also be part of a global group of teams led by Manchester City, all under the same ownership.

MAKING AN ENTRANCE

On May 21, 2013, New York City Football Club was officially announced as the 20th team in MLS. It was set to take the field for the 2015 season. At first, the club had no official colors or logo. In 2014, the club unveiled its official colors of sky blue, navy blue, and white. Sky blue is the main color of Manchester City, while the Yankees wear navy.

The NYCFC logo covers the home plate area at Yankee Stadium during soccer matches.

At the same time, the club proposed two possible logos. Fans voted and chose a circular logo with the letters NYC interlocking. The badge was similar to the design of the city's subway tokens. It was a uniquely New York logo for a club that played in New York City.

The club wanted to make sure it had experienced people finding and coaching the players. It signed Claudio Reyna as its director of football operations. Reyna had played for Manchester City and also had been the captain of the US men's national team. He had been serving as the technical director for the US youth national program.

For head coach, Reyna hired Jason Kreis, who was a former MLS Most Valuable Player (MVP). As coach of Real Salt Lake, Kreis led the scrappy underdogs to their first MLS Cup title in 2009.

When it came time to build NYCFC's roster, Reyna started with a bang. The first player the club signed was David Villa, a longtime international star and World Cup winner with Spain. Villa signed in June 2014, months before NYCFC even took the field. In July, legendary English midfielder Frank Lampard agreed to join the club.

Injuries and a contract dispute delayed Lampard's debut in 2015. But Villa was there from the start, scoring a goal in the team's first win on March 15, 2015. A crowd of 43,507 fans was on hand that day in Yankee Stadium to welcome pro soccer back to the Big Apple.

David Villa talks with young players at a clinic he held shortly after signing with NYCFC.

CHAPTER 3

SKY BLUE
MEN

Few strikers anywhere in the world were as prolific in the 2000s as David Villa. The Spaniard had starred for some of the biggest teams in his home country, including Barcelona. He also helped Spain win the European title in 2008, followed by a World Cup title in 2010. So his signing with NYCFC in the summer of 2014 certainly made news. Villa made it clear he was more than just a big name, though.

"I want to try and help MLS continue to grow, through playing, working hard, scoring goals and at the same time try to make New York City FC become the best team in the league," he said.

Villa lived up to that promise. His game-winner in the team's first home match was one of 18 goals he scored

David Villa fires home his first goal with NYCFC on March 15, 2015.

Frank Lampard provided leadership and experience in his two seasons with the club.

in 2015. He was the team's first All-Star, even scoring the game-winner for the MLS All-Stars in their match against England's Tottenham Hotspur.

Villa stepped up even more in 2016, scoring 23 goals and earning league Most Valuable Player (MVP) honors. In four seasons in New York, Villa scored 77 league goals, by far the most in team history. He was also a club captain and stayed in New York after retirement to start a minor league soccer team.

LIGHT THE LAMP

Frank Lampard's signing added to the excitement as fans eagerly awaited seeing their two international stars on the field. However, Lampard didn't arrive until July 2015. Even then, he was sidelined until August due to injuries. The delays frustrated some fans. They believed the team had misled them about his status. But once he finally took the field, Lampard worked to make up for lost time.

When healthy and in top form, Lampard remained an elite player. After three goals in just 10 games in 2015, Lampard upped it to 12 goals in 2016, his final season in New York. He notched the team's first hat trick and led NYCFC to its first playoff appearance.

THE BACK LINE

Consistency at the back helped NYCFC form one of the best defenses in MLS by 2019. That year NYCFC allowed just 42 goals in 34 league matches. Defenders Ronald Matarrita and Maxime Chanot started playing together in 2016. Alexander Callens joined the NYCFC back line in 2017.

Andrea Pirlo thrived in New York after starring in his native Italy.

As fans awaited Lampard's arrival in 2015, another world-class player joined the squad. Andrea Pirlo had roamed midfield for some of Italy's top clubs, including AC Milan and Juventus. He also helped lead Italy's national team to a World Cup title in 2006. He was one of the world's most gifted passers and also a brilliant free kick specialist.

Pirlo signed with NYCFC in July 2015, after the Juventus season ended. Making his debut as a substitute on July 26, Pirlo helped set up two goals in a 5–3 win. Pirlo's outstanding play for Juventus and NYCFC put him in the conversation for that year's Ballon d'Or, awarded to the best player in the world. But his great play did not result in a playoff spot, frustrating fans who thought the trio of Villa, Lampard, and Pirlo would produce better results.

NYCFC did make the playoffs in Pirlo's last two seasons with the club. But the boys in blue lost each time in the conference semifinals. After the 2017 season, Pirlo retired from pro soccer.

KEEPERS

Throughout its first several seasons, NYCFC's net was usually manned by one of two players. Josh Saunders was there for the start. Saunders was already a longtime MLS veteran by 2015. He debuted with the LA Galaxy in 2005 and won two MLS Cups.

Saunders brought a steady veteran presence to the new NYCFC team. He led the league in saves, helping bail out a defense playing together for the first time. Saunders started 66 games in two seasons before being traded to Orlando City.

Sean Johnson was ready to step up when NYCFC was looking for a new goalkeeper.

Sean Johnson then picked up the starting job. A steady starter for the Chicago Fire since 2010, Johnson was able to step right in and display top form. In his first four seasons, he posted 31 shutouts, and he led all goalies in saves in 2020.

THE PLAYMAKERS

After Villa retired in 2018, the captain's armband was available. Midfielder Alexander Ring put it on. Ring had been with NYCFC since 2017 after coming over from the German second division. The Finland national teamer proved to be a valuable part of the NYCFC midfield right away. He made 29 starts in his first season.

Ring was named NYCFC's Newcomer of the Year for 2017. Though not a flashy player like Pirlo, he was a vital part of the offense, setting up forwards to score. He was also a beloved teammate, evidenced by his selection as captain. Ring maintained that honor until being traded before the 2021 season.

TOMMY McNAMARA

Born and raised in West Nyack, New York, midfielder Tommy McNamara joined NYCFC in 2015 and became a fan favorite. Playing alongside some of the league's biggest stars, McNamara didn't always stand out. However, his consistent and smart play proved key for NYCFC in the early years. McNamara scored 13 goals and had 14 assists in 86 regular-season games with NYCFC from 2015 to 2018.

Maximiliano Moralez overcomes his small stature with elite field vision and passing skills.

Maximiliano Moralez's career had taken him from his native Argentina to Russia, Italy, and Mexico before he finally landed in New York City in 2017 as a Designated Player. Moralez did not get the same headlines as teammates like Villa and Pirlo, but he soon became one of the best playmakers in MLS.

Standing just 5-foot-3, Moralez was a speedy and creative player. In 2019 he became an All-Star and led the league with 20 assists. That earned him a new contract, keeping "Maxi" in sky blue for two more years.

On the receiving end of a lot of those assists was forward Héber Araujo dos Santos. After playing for three seasons in Croatia, the Brazilian burst onto the MLS scene by leading NYCFC in goals in 2019. Héber proved to be a mobile and versatile forward, able to score from any part of the field.

Alexandru Mitriță joined Héber in leading the NYCFC scoring attack. The Romanian chipped in 12 goals of his own in 2019, helping NYCFC lead the Eastern Conference in scoring. One year later it was Argentinian Valentín Castellanos topping the team's scoring list. The days of big-name superstars appeared to be over, but behind talented young players NYCFC continued to compete with the best in MLS.

NEW YORK
MOMENTS

The 43,507 fans at Yankee Stadium on March 15, 2015, got their money's worth. NYCFC began winning hearts in New York City by scoring its first win, a 2–0 shutout of the New England Revolution at Yankee Stadium. David Villa, the fledgling club's biggest star, scored the first goal, and the future looked bright.

But that would be NYCFC's last win until June. An 11-game winless streak cooled down a lot of excitement and had fans worried. NYCFC hung around the edge of the playoff race, but the club was eliminated with three straight losses to end the season.

A year that started with a lot of promise ended with a thud. The team had high hopes for experienced coach

Yankee Stadium was reconfigured to host soccer in NYCFC's first season.

YANKEE STADIUM
Armitron
pepsi
GATORADE G
5:11 PM
MetLife メットライフ
Bank of America
Ford
Go Further
att.yankees.com
DELTA
CASIO
HESS
Ford
Go Further
ETIHAD
AIRWAYS
TOYOTA
DKNY
SAP
MODELL'S
ETIHAD
AIRWAYS
BOOK NOW AT ETIHAD.COM
Heineken
NEW YORK CITY
FOOTBALL CLUB

Jack Harrison had a big impact in his first professional season.

Jason Kreis. But Kreis was fired days after the end of the season. Failing to make the playoffs despite having a world-class trio of players in David Villa, Andrea Pirlo, and Frank Lampard proved to be too much for ownership to overlook.

VIEIRA TURNS THINGS AROUND

The team then turned to another world-class talent to help turn things around. Only this time, it was as a coach, not a player. Patrick Vieira had been one of the world's best playmakers as a pro in England and Italy, as well as for France's national team. In retirement he joined the front office of Manchester City, and then NYCFC gave him his first head coaching job.

Vieira got help from rookie midfielder Jack Harrison, the first pick in the draft. Harrison helped distribute the ball to Villa, who had an MVP season. Pirlo was also effective in midfield, and Lampard chipped in 12 goals, despite being limited due to injury. Players enjoyed playing for Vieira, and the results showed on the field.

On the last day of the regular season, Harrison and Villa both scored as NYCFC hammered the Columbus Crew 4–1. NYCFC clinched second place in the East after finishing in eighth place the year before. That meant an automatic spot in the conference semifinals, where it would face Toronto FC.

On the road for the first leg, NYCFC was locked in a defensive battle. Despite playing well, the defense allowed two goals after the 83rd minute, leaving a 2–0 deficit to overcome in the second leg. Instead, back in the Bronx, NYCFC fell apart

David Villa represented NYCFC in the 2017 All-Star Game, when the MLS team faced Real Madrid.

in a 5–0 defeat. Despite the setback, Vieira was confident the team would be back the next year.

ANOTHER GO

The 2017 home opener showed what was old and new about NYCFC. Villa scored two goals, the start of another strong year for him. Maxi Moralez, taking up Lampard's role after the Englishman departed, also scored in a 4–0 shutout of DC United. Sean Johnson, who had taken over in goal for Josh Saunders, posted the clean sheet.

After a possession-based, attacking approach helped NYCFC challenge for the best record in MLS in 2016, Vieira stuck with it and had similar results in 2017. A highlight for fans was Villa's hat trick against the Red Bulls to win a second consecutive Hudson River Derby.

NYCFC again entered the playoffs at the conference semifinals, and the club again had a letdown. The Blues allowed a sixth-minute goal against Columbus and went on to lose the first leg 4–1. They returned home needing a miracle.

NYCFC got some early hope when Villa converted a penalty in the 16th minute. Then early in the second half, Andraž Struna doubled the lead. NYCFC needed just one more goal to tie the aggregate score. In the 66th minute, Harrison had a one-on-one but fired it right at the keeper. Four minutes later, Rodney Wallace hit the post. NYCFC went down, but it went down fighting.

BIG CHANGES

NYCFC's core of world stars helped make the team competitive immediately. But as those players aged and retired, the club found itself in need of a major overhaul. After Lampard's 2016 departure, Pirlo was the next to leave. He retired after the 2017 season. The club made a lot more moves that year, with 11 players departing from the 2017 team. Vieira also left midway through 2018 to take a job in his native France.

Still, the club had Villa, who had another strong season. But after another conference semifinal defeat, he signed with a team in Japan. That offseason saw even more changes, including the departures of Wallace and Tommy McNamara. In came high-scoring forwards Alexandru Mitriță and Héber. The club retained coach Domènec Torrent, who had replaced Vieira.

Despite the loss of its all-time leading scorer in Villa, NYCFC had its best season yet in 2019. The club set team records with 63 goals scored and 42 goals allowed. It posted the best record in the Eastern Conference for the first time.

Frustrations boiled over for Harrison and NYCFC in the 2017 playoff loss to Columbus.

Sean Johnson makes a big save in the 2019 playoffs against Toronto.

The club earned a fourth straight appearance in the conference semifinals. Once again, Toronto FC was the opponent. But this time it was a single knockout game. Toronto started out dominating, but Johnson made four first-half saves to keep the Blues in the game.

Toronto scored just after halftime, but Ismael Tajouri-Shradi tied it for NYCFC. However, in the final minutes of the game, Ronald Matarrita made an illegal tackle in the box. Toronto converted the penalty kick to send NYCFC to what might have been its most heartbreaking playoff loss yet.

After the season, Ronny Deila was named the new coach. The club returned almost all its scoring, its core of defenders, and its goalkeeper. However, every team's best-laid plans went out the window in 2020, when the COVID-19 pandemic disrupted the league and ultimately kept most fans out of the stadiums. Despite these challenges, NYCFC earned its fifth playoff berth in a row as the fifth seed in the east. However, it fell to Orlando City in a shootout in the first round. The playoffs had become a yearly expectation in New York. A championship remained a dream.

OPEN CUP WOES

It would be easy for NYCFC fans to forget about the US Open Cup each year. The club struggled to find its footing in the tournament, which is open to all men's teams in the United States. NYCFC failed to win a match in its first four seasons of existence. It finally broke through in 2019, actually winning two matches and reaching the quarterfinals before falling to Orlando City in a penalty shootout.

TIMELINE

2013	2014	2015	2015	2016
MLS announces on May 21 that New York City FC will join the league in 2015.	NYCFC announces on June 2 that star forward David Villa of Spain would join the club. Additional big-name signings Andrea Pirlo and Frank Lampard follow.	NYCFC draws with fellow expansion team Orlando City 1–1 on March 8 in its first game.	On November 9, former France captain Patrick Vieira is named as NYCFC's head coach, replacing Jason Kreis.	Jack Harrison and Villa each score on July 3 as NYCFC beats the Red Bulls 2–0 to claim its first win in the Hudson River Derby.

2016	2017	2018	2019	2020
NYCFC goes 15–10–9 to qualify for the MLS playoffs for the first time. Villa is named MLS MVP after his 23-goal season.	Villa scores 22 goals as NYCFC finishes with the second-best record in MLS.	Domènec Torrent, a longtime respected assistant coach, is hired as head coach on June 11 to replace Vieira, who left for a job in France.	With Villa gone, Maximiliano Moralez leads NYCFC to the Eastern Conference semifinals for the fourth year in a row.	In a season disrupted by COVID-19, NYCFC makes the playoffs for the fifth year in a row but loses to Orlando City in the first round.

TEAM FACTS

FIRST SEASON

2015

STADIUM

Yankee Stadium (2015–)

KEY PLAYERS

Alexander Callens (2017–)
Valentín Castellanos (2018–)
Jack Harrison (2016–17)
Héber (2019–)
Sean Johnson (2017–)
Frank Lampard (2015–16)
Tommy McNamara (2015–18)
Jesús Medina (2018–)
Alexandru Mitriță (2019–20)
Maximiliano Moralez (2017–)
Andrea Pirlo (2015–17)
Alexander Ring (2017–20)
David Villa (2015–18)

KEY COACHES

Jason Kreis (2015)
Patrick Vieira (2016–18)
Domènec Torrent (2018–19)
Ronny Delia (2020–)

MLS MOST VALUABLE PLAYER

David Villa (2016)

GLOSSARY

assists
Passes that lead directly to a goal.

clean sheet
A shutout.

corner kick
A free kick from a corner of the field near the opponent's goal.

Designated Player
An MLS player whose salary counts outside the salary cap, allowing teams to sign stars.

expansion team
A new team that is added to an existing league.

free kick
An unguarded kick awarded to a team after an opponent's foul.

knockout
A kind of competition in which one loss eliminates a team.

leg
One of two matches in a series.

penalty area
The box in front of the goal where a player is granted a penalty kick if he or she is fouled.

supporters' groups
Fan groups that stand and cheer for their team throughout the game by singing, chanting, drumming, waving flags, and more.

tackle
An attempt to take the ball away from an opponent.

MORE INFORMATION

BOOKS

Dyer, Kristian R. *New York Red Bulls*. Minneapolis, MN: Abdo Publishing, 2022.

Kortemeier, Todd. *Total Soccer*. Minneapolis, MN: Abdo Publishing, 2017.

Marthaler, Jon. *Ultimate Soccer Road Trip*. Minneapolis, MN: Abdo Publishing, 2019.

ONLINE RESOURCES

To learn more about New York City FC, please visit **abdobooklinks.com** or scan this QR code. These links are routinely monitored and updated to provide the most current information available.

INDEX

ABOUT THE AUTHOR

Anthony K. Hewson has followed American soccer since before the MLS days. Originally from San Diego, he now lives in the Bay Area with his wife and dogs.